W9-ADJ-046

Why Can't I Learn Like Everyone Else?

Youth with Learning Disabilities

A House Between Homes
Youth in the Foster Care System

A Different Way of Seeing
Youth with Visual Impairments and Blindness

The Ocean Inside
Youth Who Are Deaf and Hard of Hearing

My Name Is Not Slow
Youth with Mental Retardation

Chained
Youth with Chronic Illness

Runaway Train
Youth with Emotional Disturbance

Stuck on Fast Forward
Youth with Attention-Deficit/Hyperactivity Disorder

Why Can't I Learn Like Everyone Else?
Youth with Learning Disabilities

Finding My Voice
Youth with Speech Impairment

Somebody Hear Me Crying
Youth in Protective Services

Guaranteed Rights
The Legislation That Protects Youth with Special Needs

The Journey Toward Recovery
Youth with Brain Injury

Breaking Down Barriers
Youth with Physical Challenges

On the Edge of Disaster
Youth in the Juvenile Court System

The Hidden Child
Youth with Autism

Why Can't I Learn Like Everyone Else?

Youth with Learning Disabilities

BY SHIRLEY BRINKERHOFF

MASON CREST PUBLISHERS

LIBRARY
FRANKLIN PIERCE COLLEGE
RINDGE, NH 03461

Mason Crest Publishers Inc.
370 Reed Road
Broomall, Pennsylvania 19008
(866) MCP-BOOK (toll free)

Copyright © 2004 by Mason Crest Publishers. All rights reserved. No part of this publication may be reproduced or transmitted in any form or by any means, electronic or mechanical, including photocopying, recording, taping, or any information storage and retrieval system, without permission from the publisher.

First printing
1 2 3 4 5 6 7 8 9 10

Brinkerhoff, Shirley.
Why can't I learn like everyone else? : youth with learning disabilities / Shirley Brinkerhoff.
v. cm.—(Youth with special needs)
Includes bibliographical references and index.
Contents: Changes—Learning to get by—Anger—Another world—Conflicts—Tensions—The power of persistence—Hope.
1. Learning disabled youth—Education—United States—Juvenile literature. 2. Learning disabilities—United States—Juvenile literature. [1. Learning disabilities.] I. Title. II. Series.
LC4705.B74 2004
371.9'0973—dc22   2003018438

ISBN 1-59084-730-X
1-59084-727-X (series)

Design by Harding House Publishing Service.
Composition by Bytheway Publishing Services, Inc., Binghamton, New York.
Cover art by Keith Rosko.
Cover design by Benjamin Stewart.
Produced by Harding House Publishing Service, Vestal, New York.
Printed and bound in the Hashemite Kingdom of Jordan.

Picture credits: Benjamin Stewart: pp. 16, 36, 37, 90; Dover, *Dictionary of American Portraits*: p. 118; Eyewire: pp. 38, 115; Photo Alto: pp. 19, 21, 22, 23, 25, 34, 35, 39, 41, 44, 57, 83; PhotoDisc: pp. 17, 18, 26, 40, 42, 45, 46, 54, 55, 56, 60, 69, 70, 71, 73, 74, 88, 89, 98, 99, 100, 102, 110, 111, 112, 113, 116; Stockbyte: p. 59. Individuals in the photographs supplied by Eyewire, Photo Alto, PhotoDisc, and Stockbyte are models, and these images are for illustrative purposes only.

CONTENTS

A child with special needs is not defined by his disability.
It is just one part of who he is.

Introduction

E ach child is unique and wonderful. And some children have differences we call special needs. Special needs can mean many things. Sometimes children will learn differently, or hear with an aid, or read with Braille. A young person may have a hard time communicating or paying attention. A child can be born with a special need, or acquire it by an accident or through a health condition. Sometimes a child will be developing in a typical manner and then become delayed in that development. But whatever problems a child may have with her learning, emotions, behavior, or physical body, she is always a person first. She is not defined by her disability; instead, the disability is just one part of who she is.

Inclusion means that young people with and without special needs are together in the same settings. They learn together in school; they play together in their communities; they all have the same opportunities to belong. Children learn so much from each other. A child with a hearing impairment, for example, can teach another child a new way to communicate using sign language. Someone else who has a physical disability affecting his legs can show his friends how to play wheelchair basketball. Children with and without special needs can teach each other how to appreciate and celebrate their differences. They can also help each other discover how people are more alike than they are different. Understanding and appreciating how we all have similar needs helps us learn empathy and sensitivity.

In this series, you will read about young people with special needs from the unique perspectives of children and adolescents who are experiencing the disability firsthand. Of course, not all children with a particular disability are the same as the characters in the stories. But the stories demonstrate at an emotional level how a special need impacts a child, his family, and his friends. The factual material in each chapter will expand your horizons by adding to your knowledge about a particular disability. The series as a whole will help you understand differences better and appreciate how they make us all stronger and better.

—*Cindy Croft*
Educational Consultant

YOUTH WITH SPECIAL NEEDS provides a unique forum for demystifying a wide variety of childhood medical and developmental disabilities. Written to captivate an adolescent audience, the books bring to life the challenges and triumphs experienced by children with common chronic conditions such as hearing loss, mental retardation, physical differences, and speech difficulties. The topics are addressed frankly through a blend of fiction and fact. Students and teachers alike can move beyond the information provided by accessing the resources offered at the end of each text.

This series is particularly important today as the number of children with special needs is on the rise. Over the last two decades, advances in pediatric medical techniques have allowed children who have chronic illnesses and disabilities to live longer, more functional lives. As a result, these children represent an increasingly visible part of North American population in all aspects of daily life. Students are exposed to peers with special needs in their classrooms, through extracurricular activities, and in the community. Often, young people have misperceptions and unanswered questions about a child's disabilities—and more important, his or her *abilities*. Many times, there is no vehicle for talking about these complex issues in a comfortable manner.

This series provides basic information that will leave readers with a deeper understanding of each condition, along with an awareness of some of the associated emotional impacts on affected children, their families, and their peers. It will also encourage further conversation about these issues. Most important, the series promotes a greater comfort for its readers as they live, play, and work side by side with these individuals who have medical and developmental differences—youth with special needs.

—Dr. Lisa Albers, Dr. Carolyn Bridgemohan, Dr. Laurie Glader
Medical Consultants

All things are continually
being born of change. . . .
—Marcus Aurelius

1

CHANGES

It's funny how when one thing in your life changes everything else ends up changing, too.

When I was little, I used to stand those little black dominoes up in a long row. Sometimes I made the row curvy like a mountain road; sometimes I made it straight. But whenever I pushed that first domino down, I knew all the other dominoes were going down, too. That's kind of how it was when I found out my dad was marrying Janet. I had my life all arranged, sort of like those dominoes.

Then Janet came along, and that was the first domino falling.

Then she discovered my secret, and all the rest of the dominoes went down, too.

That probably doesn't make much sense to you. And it won't until I tell you something about me. My name is Charlie Begay, and there are two things you need to know right from the beginning:

I'm a Navajo. That's the first thing, and it's important to me. My family has lived in this area for more years than you can count, near the Animas River in the northwest part of New Mexico. If you stand on the brown hills behind our house and look north, you can see the San Juan Mountains up near Durango, Colorado, about thirty miles (48.3 kilometers) away. Those mountains are so high that some are covered with snow for nine or ten months of the year. All my life I've been telling myself that I'm going to ski those mountains some day, up at Purgatory Ski Resort. Sometimes, when things are really bad in school—which is most of the time—I close my eyes and

UNDERSTANDING LEARNING DISORDERS

There are several different ways to define learning disorders.

According to Stanley S. Lamm, M.D., and Martin L. Fisch, Ph.D., in their book, *Learning Disabilities Explained*, a learning disorder "describes a condition or a series of specific conditions that interfere with the normal learning process in a child who is of average or above average intelligence."

Paula Anne Ford-Martin ("Learning Disorders," in the *Gale Encyclopedia of Medicine*), writes that learning disorders involve difficulties with how we acquire information, how we retain information, and how we process information.

Melvin D. Levine, one of the foremost learning experts in America, explains that the term "learning disorder" refers to achievement at levels substantially below those expected for a student's "age, amount of schooling, and level of

A student with a learning disability may get one-on-one help with a special education teacher in a resource room.

Despite impaired brain function in some areas, youth with learning disabilities have average or above-average intelligence.

intelligence." Although such students have average or above average intelligence, they also have some impaired brain function that prevents them from making at least average academic progress.

Learning disorders appear in many different forms and affect different aspects of learning. They most commonly affect the ability to learn to read, write, and spell—**dyslexia**, to do mathematics—**dyscalculia**, and to write—**dysgraphia**. The best-known learning disorder is dyslexia. This word comes from combining the prefix "dys," which means *difficulty*, and "lexia," which means *language* or *words*. (For more on dyslexia, see chapter 2.)

There are many ways to learn. Students with learning disabilities may do better with hands-on activities than they do with books or paper-and-pencil exercises.

Dr. Levine, however, divides learning problems into six categories:

1. language disorders
2. attention deficits
3. memory disorders
4. motor weaknesses
5. spatial or sequencing difficulties
6. higher order thinking deficiencies

WHO HAS LEARNING DISORDERS?

Most educators estimate the number of children in the United States diagnosed with learning disorders at about five percent. Others, however, believe that as many as 15 to 20 percent have learning disorders, even though the disorders might not be recognized or diagnosed.

Learning disorders occur in all ethnic and socioeconomic groups. However, they are often more apt to be noticed when a child has other challenges to overcome. For instance, Charlie Begay may have more problems with school and reading because he may have grown up in a home that had few resources and where the people around him may

A child with a learning disorder may have difficulty learning to recognize letters.

have spoken English as a second language. The fact that his father cannot read either means that he had no reading role models or mentors when he was small. Sometimes, though, children who come from another cultural background or from a home with few economic resources are misdiagnosed—they may appear to have a learning disorder, when really they have just never had the opportunity to learn skills that other segments of the population have.

Learning disorders do tend to run in families. If a parent has a learning disability, his or her children are more apt to have one too. It may be that Charlie's father also has a learning disability.

HOW ARE LEARNING DISORDERS DIAGNOSED?

Public schools are required to provide special education for students with learning disorders. (For more information, see chapter 6.) However, it can be difficult for teachers, doctors, and researchers to agree on an accepted definition of which learning problems are actually authentic disorders and require special educational services.

Generally, learning disorders are identified by tests (which federal law requires public school systems to give free of charge) that show a difference between a student's intelligence and achievement levels. It is not always simple, however, to make this assessment. For example, in the case of dyslexia, one of the most familiar learning disorders, more than just a single test is needed to prove the disorder is present. Many tests are given in order to measure oral and written language—both expressive and receptive. Other tests are given to measure intellectual functioning, educational achievement, and cognitive processing.

The professionals who evaluate these tests must then determine whether or not an apparent learning disorder is

Students with learning disorders need opportunities to interact with other children their age.

related to other disorders and conditions that might also be present. These could include mental retardation, ADHD (attention-deficit/hyperactivity disorder), anxiety, depression, developmental disorders, physical or sensory impairments, and numerous other factors that could contribute to learning problems. This can make the diagnosis of a learning disorder a complex task.

Professionals often use well-known tests such as the Woodcock-Johnson Psychoeducational Battery and the Wechsler Intelligence Scale for Children to aid in the process of diagnosis.

THE LEGAL RIGHTS OF CHILDREN WITH LEARNING DISORDERS

Since 1973, a series of federal and state laws and court decisions have supported the rights of individuals with

A child who has trouble reading may excel at art or some other skill.

Learning activities that require manipulating objects manually may help some students to grasp concepts more easily. This is just one educational strategy that may help youth with learning disorders.

disabilities to fully participate in all aspects of our society. Section 504 of the Rehabilitation Act of 1973, a civil rights law, prohibits the **discrimination** of individuals with disabilities, and provides **due process** where discrimination might have occurred. The Americans with Disabilities Act, signed by President Bush in 1992, calls for the "full inclusion" of individuals with disabilities in all aspects of our society, including transportation, telecommunications, and education. It is not the intent of these laws to provide unfair advantage, but what they do provide is equal access— "reasonable accommodations" for individuals who are "otherwise qualified."

In 1975, the 94th Congress, passed the landmark Education for the Handicapped Act, known as Public Law 94-142. This law was recently re-authorized as the Individuals with Disabilities Education Act (IDEA); it provides states with federal monies to serve the needs of children with disabilities. This is achieved through a very specific process defined within that law. All preschool and school-age students, regardless of the severity of their disability, must be provided an "appropriate education" in the "least restrictive environment." A multidisciplinary team, which includes the parent, conducts an evaluation that identifies a student's eligibility and needs, and uses an individualized education plan (IEP) to describe a program that meets that student's needs. To ensure that the educational program is appropriate to the child's current (and evolving) needs, programs must be reviewed at least annually, with periodic reevaluations conducted at least every three years.

RECOGNIZING GIFTS

People with dyslexia often have problems with their self-image. In a world where reading is so important, they

Schools need to create atmospheres where discrimination against students with learning disorders does not exist.

feel as though they will never be able to "measure up." They face problems with language in areas including translating language into thought (such as in listening or reading), or translating thought into language (such as in writing or speaking)—and these problems place them at a disadvantage in twenty-first century North American society.

At the same time, however, many people with dyslexia show unusual abilities in other areas of life, including art,

A student with a learning disorder may struggle as hard to decipher ordinary letters as though they were a secret code.

music, athletics, drama, and architecture. Charlie Begay is an example of this. Although he struggles to decode letters and words on the pages of a book, he is physically strong and athletic, and also has some artistic talent.

People with dyslexia and other learning disorders are valuable members of our world, with much to offer. They frequently learn how to emphasize their strengths and downplay areas of weakness.

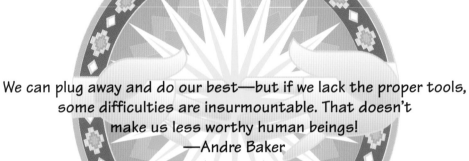

We can plug away and do our best—but if we lack the proper tools,
some difficulties are insurmountable. That doesn't
make us less worthy human beings!
—Andre Baker

2

LEARNING TO GET BY

By second grade, I knew I'd never catch up with the other kids. They were already reading chapter books, with real stories. I wasn't even good enough to be in the bottom reading group by then—I had to leave the room and go with a reading tutor every day during reading time.

The tutor was supposed to help me, I guess. But he just kept sounding out the words over and over with me in this bored way, like I would finally catch on if he did it a thousand times or so. I never even tried to tell him about the words moving around on the page.

Things were actually getting worse instead of better. In second grade, you have to read other subjects, like social studies. And if I couldn't even read the simple little reading book, how was I supposed to read *other* books? Nobody told me what to do about that, and I couldn't figure out who to ask.

I could recognize a lot of short words, but the reading just kept getting harder: Number one, the words were longer. Number two, there were a lot more words on each page now and I kept losing my place. They used to let me use my finger to point to the word I was on, but by second grade, you're not supposed to do that anymore.

Another problem was that report cards are different in second grade. In first grade, we just got an S for satisfactory and a U for unsatisfactory. I made sure I behaved myself so that I got an S in just about everything. When I got a U in reading, I just told my dad I'd try to do better. He never said too much.

But in second grade, letter grades started showing up on my report card, and even my dad can tell a D and an F from an A. *That* was a problem. So were the notes the second-grade teacher wrote on the report card. As far as I could make out, they were about how I needed extra help, and Dad should take me to a "something"—but there she put in these big long words that I couldn't figure out. Since Dad couldn't read the note, I just told him the note said the teacher was proud of me, and he looked really happy.

In third grade, my teacher, Mrs. Rice, sent home notes, too, only she wanted me to bring them back, signed by my dad. Even though my dad can't read, he knows how to sign his name, so I always told him the notes were about things like field trips or projects, and he always signed. A couple of times, Mrs. Rice asked me about the notes.

"So when is your father coming in to see me, Charlie?" she would say.

"Coming in?" I asked, feeling panicky.

"Remember that note I sent home last week? Asking him to call me and set up a meeting? He never called."

"Oh," I said, wishing more than ever that I was smart so I could figure out what to do here. "He's been really busy this week, Mrs. Rice. I'm sure he'll call really soon, though."

Mrs. Rice had this way of pushing her lips together in a tight line, like she wasn't real happy about what I said.

One time when I brought back one of her notes, signed, she said, "Oh, good, now we can set up the tests."

I didn't like the sound of that, but I didn't know what to do about it, either. So I just waited. Later that week, a man I'd never seen before came and took me out of class. He made me go with him to a special room with a table and some chairs, and I had to answer a lot of questions and work some things that were kind of like puzzles—except they weren't any fun.

Some of the puzzles were made out of wood blocks and beads

and stuff, and the man would build something with them, then take it apart and ask me to build it again, exactly the way he had. Each time I finished, he'd glance at his watch, and then write down words in his notebook.

Next, he showed me pictures of things like squares and circles and weird shapes and let me look at them for a certain amount of time. Then he'd take the picture away and ask me to draw it from memory.

After that, he asked me about a million questions, like these:

"Do you feel that reading is hard for you?"

"Do you often feel that you don't understand what you are reading?"

"Do you have trouble sounding out words?"

"By the time you reach the end of a paragraph, do you forget what you read at the beginning of the paragraph?"

By the time he asked about a hundred of those questions, I just started answering yes every time, since that was almost always the right answer anyway.

A few days after that test, Mrs. Rice sent home another note to my father. This time, I just threw the note away. "He didn't want to sign it," I told Mrs. Rice the next day. She looked unhappy, but then a few days later she told me I was getting a new tutor—"just for the time being"—one who would help me with more than just my reading.

But I didn't meet alone with her, like I had with the first one. Instead, there were three other kids who came, too, and they were all *first-graders*. Picture this: every day during reading, three first-graders walked right past the open door of my classroom. And while everybody in my class was watching, I had to get up and follow the first-graders down the hall to the Resource Room. That alone was enough to ruin my day, every single time.

But it got worse.

Once we were inside the Resource Room, I discovered that I couldn't even read as well as the first-graders. It was obvious what the tutor thought of me when she found that out. After she worked with the first-graders for a couple of months, they got a lot better; even I could see that. But I just stayed the same, no matter what she did. After a while, she pretty much stopped calling on me.

Mrs. Rice gave me another note to give my father, but I threw that one away too. Something about those notes scared me.

"He won't sign it," I told Mrs. Rice.

She shook her head and looked unhappy, but after that, I stopped going to the Resource Room. One day I saw her talking to the man who had asked me all the questions. I tried to hear what they were saying, but all I caught was, ". . . he needs to be classified." I didn't like the sound of that.

Just a couple of days after that, though, Mrs. Rice got sick and had to go into the hospital. She didn't come back for the rest of the year, and the substitute didn't seem to worry about getting me "classified," whatever that meant. So I breathed a sigh of relief.

But now, I had to handle my schoolwork all by myself. That was when I knew I had to take matters into my own hands. And that's also when Jake moved in next door.

We were friends from the start. There's a church parking lot across the street from my house, where I go just about every day to skateboard. Jake's parents were still hauling boxes into their house from their pickup truck when he saw me there.

I didn't really notice him at first, because when I skateboard, I don't think about anything else. Skateboarding is one of the only times I don't feel dumb, then and when I am drawing or out in the hills with Dad watching the animals and birds. I was still learning to do an Ollie back then, where you slam the back of the board down with your foot and the board goes up in the air, and that was the first day I really landed one.

And here came this spindly little kid running across the parking lot toward me, yelling, "Hey! Teach me to do that!"

That was Jake. He didn't have a skateboard or a helmet or anything—his parents said they couldn't afford it because Jake has five brothers and twin sisters, and it's all they can handle just to feed eight kids.

So I let Jake use my stuff, and after that he started hanging out at my house a lot. He said seven "siblings" were about six too many for him. That's the kind of words Jake uses—*siblings*—instead of just saying brothers and sisters. But he likes it at my house since there's usually nobody home but me. Jake likes the day-old cupcakes Dad brings home too. Those and the day-old donuts. Dad told me once he worries that Jake is so little because he doesn't always get enough to eat, with all those brothers and sisters. So he makes sure he brings home snacks Jake likes.

Jake didn't do too well as the new kid at Corando. The other kids teased him because he's the shortest in our class and he's always the first one out in dodge ball. Also, he can't make a basket to save his life and he stinks at math. But I could see right away that he was really good at reading. So Jake and me, we worked out the deal I told you about: I'd teach him everything I knew about skateboarding and other sports and help him do his math, because I can work out the problems in my head. He'd help me do all the other homework, and I give him a dollar a page when I have it. We also discovered that I can remember just about everything I hear in class, so when we do our homework together, we both do okay.

That was four and a half years ago, and our deal's been working out fine ever since. Jake's still kind of slow on the skateboard, but I just keep teaching him. And I've managed to get through all the grades without being held back, so far.

Somehow, our deal doesn't seem like cheating. It feels more like what my dad calls "bartering." Like when, instead of paying the barber who gives us haircuts, Dad changes the oil in his truck for him. I figure Jake and I are *bartering*. It also keeps my dad from being really disappointed with me.

I used to worry, sometimes, about what would happen if people discovered my secret. But our bartering was working okay, at least until Janet came into the picture and discovered I couldn't read. Like I told you, that was when the first domino went down.

IDENTIFYING A LEARNING DISABILITY

Usually, parents play an important role in identifying a learning disability. If parents suspect their child has a learning disorder, diagnosis is the first step toward treatment. Since these disorders are most obvious in school settings, poor achievement in a particular subject is usually the first indication of a problem.

Sometimes, as in Charlie's case, parents are unaware that their child has a problem. Sooner or later, however, teachers at school will notice that a student is having difficulty. An otherwise bright kid will become more and more frustrated in math class. Or a child may do well when tested on material that she heard, and yet fall further and further behind whenever she is required to read material. When this happens, the teacher will usually make a referral to the school psychologist, requesting that the child be tested. Before testing can take place, however, the parent or legal guardian must sign a permission letter. The school will try to involve

Students with learning disorders may spend part of their day working in small groups with a special education teacher.

Identifying a learning disorder is the first step toward helping that child succeed in school.

Computers often provide another learning media for students with learning disorders.

the parents as much as possible in the entire process of evaluation, diagnosis, and placement. Nothing can take place without the parent's permission.

Federal laws guarantee each child a free and "appropriate" education. Each state and school system has their own procedure for carrying out these laws, but Public Law 94-142 guarantees that the following steps will take place:

1. **Search.** Each school system will have a procedure for identifying students who might have a disability. This means that parents and teachers can refer a child they suspect may have a learning disorder to the school psychologist for diagnostic testing.
2. **Find.** Once a student with a potential problem has been identified, a system is in place for collecting information and designing an evaluation.
3. **Evaluation.** A comprehensive and multidisciplinary evaluation should be done. This will involve the

school psychologist as well as teachers and other school personnel.

4. **Conference.** Parents or guardians meet with school personnel to review the evaluation conclusions, any labels or diagnoses established, any proposed placement, and the individualized education plan (IEP). All this should be recorded in writing.

5. **Parents' decision process.** Parents or guardians decide to accept, request explanations or changes, or reject the proposed placement and IEP.

6. **Appeals process.** If parents reject the label or diagnosis, placement recommendation, or IEP, an appeals process starts with the local school and can go from there to the county or state level.

7. **Follow-up.** Progress reports are provided to the family, and a formal reevaluation is done every three years (or sooner if requested by parents or teachers). Steps 5 and 6 are then repeated before implementing the next year's plans.

Children with various learning difficulties enjoy art activities.

Classified

When a student is "classified," that means the school system has formally identified this child as having a particular handicapping condition. Being classified then entitles that child to certain education services.

Each student, however, will continue to have individual characteristics with unique strengths and needs. A classification should never be perceived as a label that defines that person.

DIFFERENT KINDS OF LEARNING DISORDERS

Language Disorders

Language disorders are among the most common of the learning disorders, and cover a wide range of difficulties, both in understanding and in expressing ideas. While some students may not be able to grasp the meaning of individual words, others may struggle to comprehend sentences spoken by others (and may be especially confused by long or complex sentences), or to organize their own thoughts into sentences.

A student with a language disorder may struggle to organize his thoughts into sentences.

A child with a learning disorder may hide her disability by never raising her hand to answer a question.

"Parents," says Dr. Mel Levine, "should be aware that language is all-consuming in the everyday existence of their children."

Language is how humans communicate with each other—and even with animals. Language disorders negatively impact thinking, reading, spelling, writing, and even mathematics. Social relationships are affected by a person's ability, or inability, to use language; a child who cannot communicate with other children is unlikely to form friendships. Our society, and especially our schools, are set up in such a way that they reward students who excel in the area of language. Nonverbal thinkers, however, often face just failure.

For Charlie Begay, learning problems meant rejection from many of his peers. Because his friend Jake also struggled with learning problems—specifically in mathematics—and some motor weaknesses, the two boys were able to team up and support each other. Often, however, learning disorders mean a lonely, isolated childhood.

A young person with a learning disorder may feel discouraged, depressed, and embarrassed by his disability.

A nonverbal thinker may be just as intelligent as the student who excels at verbal skills.

A teacher is most apt to use "literate English."

Compounding the problem of language disorders is the fact that language itself is a very complex thing. Levine explains that language is made up of several different types of languages, including, *automatic, literate, concrete, abstract, receptive,* and *expressive* types. Following are brief descriptions of these different types, any or all of which may pose a problem to a student with a language disorder:

- *Automatic English:* The type of speech used at the mall, the bus stop, etc., where students speak informally and use "high-frequency vocabulary," such as *you know, like,* or *chill out.*
- *Literate English:* Used in classrooms, in academic reading and writing, and for technical terms. This language is not commonly used in everyday, familiar settings.

- *Concrete English:* This is the language of the senses, representing things people experience by feeling, seeing, hearing, smelling, and tasting. *Sour, dog, fuzzy,* and *itch* are all examples of concrete English.
- *Abstract English*: This language deals with things that can't be understood through the senses, such as ideas and concepts, and becomes increasingly important as students move into higher grades in school.
- *Receptive English:* This involves the level of understanding a child has for what he or she hears from others, including a story read by her teacher or a joke told by a friend.
- *Expressive English:* This involves a person's ability to translate his or her thoughts into messages that are then given to and understood by other people.

Reading Disorder or Dyslexia

Dyslexia is a language-based learning disorder that impairs a person's ability to read. It does not indicate a lack of intelligence; in fact, many people with dyslexia show average to above-average intelligence. Among students who receive special education services for specific learning disorders, 70 to 80 percent have problems with reading, and dyslexia is the most common diagnosis. Dyslexia affects people of both sexes (but somewhere between 60 and 80 percent of all children who have dyslexia are boys), all ethnic groups, and all socioeconomic groups. Studies show that those with this disorder actually process information in a different area of the brain than do nondyslexics.

Children with dyslexia have difficulty understanding the meaning of the words they do read; they "miss" many words altogether; and they are apt to reverse the position of some letters in certain words. (For instance, they may read "dog"

Although reading disorders affect both genders, between 60 and 80 percent of all children with dyslexia are boys.

instead of "god" or "was" instead of "saw"—or they may reverse the letters themselves and read "bab" instead of "dad.")

Mathematics Disorder

Most children who have a mathematics disorder also have a reading disorder. Children with this disorder have a hard time learning to count. Simple addition and subtraction calculations are difficult for them, and they are often unable to create a mental image of sets of objects. Many times they are also unable to think in terms of right and left, up and down, or east and west. They may have problems with sequencing things into a specific order.

Disorder of Written Expression

Children with this disorder will have a reading disorder as well, and most children with a reading disorder will also

Being sent to the board to write out a math problem may be a harrowing experience for a student with a mathematics disorder.

have a writing disorder. They will have trouble with spelling, grammar, and punctuation. Making sentences and para-graphs will be difficult for them, and they tend to write slowly and illegibly. They may have a motor disability as well that gives them problems with **fine motor coordination** in their hands, making it even more difficult for them to write neatly. Their school papers tend to be full of erasures and crossed out words. They may write their letters backward, or they may write entire words or sentences in reverse order. Although all children have these difficulties as they learn to write, the child with a disorder will continue to have trou-bles after other children her age have successfully mastered the skills necessary for writing.

Many students with learning disorders learn to compensate for their weaknesses by depending more on their strengths. This often allows them to experience a sense of achievement and success.

COMPENSATION

Compensation is a way in which people exaggerate or be-gin to depend on one of their strengths in order to make up for a weakness. In Charlie Begay's case, his excellent memory has allowed him to compensate, at least in part, for his difficulty in reading. Whatever his friend reads to him or he hears in class he remembers, allowing him to retain infor-mation needed for quizzes and tests without reading on his own.

Teachers who work with students who have learning dis-orders frequently see this type of compensation. Because those with learning disorders often have a high level of intel-ligence, it is not uncommon for them to have excellent memories or other skills that help them compensate for their disorder. Because of this type of compensation, however, learning disorders sometimes go unrecognized and undiag-nosed for years—in extreme cases, for a lifetime.

DISAPPOINTING THEIR PARENTS, DISAPPOINTING THEMSELVES

Children who do not learn in the manner and at the rate they are expected to often feel tremendous disappointment from their parents and their teachers. That feeling of being a disappointment to others can be one of the most painful aspects of having a learning disorder.

All too often, this kind of negative self-concept centered around learning leads to other problems. First, many children with learning disorders avoid the activity that is so hard for them. A child with dyscalculia (a learning disorder in mathematics) is likely to struggle with math and will often avoid math at all costs. This only leads to further problems,

For a young person with a learning disorder, a library may seem like a place that has nothing to offer. A negative self-concept can keep him from seeing the resources that are available to him.

Many students with learning disorders become discouraged with school.

however. While other students are practicing their math skills and getting better and better at them, students with dyscalculia not only have a problem with basic math but also lose out on the math skills others continue to develop on a daily basis at school and in life.

The same scenario happens with dyslexia and other learning disorders. It is no wonder, then, that many students who have learning disorders end up dropping out of school—the figure is estimated to be as high as 40 percent. In some cases, students with learning disorders end up getting into trouble with the law.

Learning Disorders and Other Problems

Social workers sometimes have to pick up the story where frustrated educators leave off. When learning disorders go undiagnosed, or when effective help is not given in school or at home, some young people give up on ever creating a meaningful life. In extreme cases, they may even turn to gangs for acceptance or to substance abuse for escape.

Alia's story showed this progression. In the earliest grades, Alia seemed to be on target academically. By the time third grade rolled around, however, she had fallen markedly behind her classmates. Although she had learned to read the simple material required of first- and second-graders, the more complex content of third-grade material—along with much longer assignments—began to take its toll. Though Alia had a fairly large number of words she recognized by sight, new ones puzzled her because she lacked a true understanding of how to use phonetics to decipher these words. To make matters worse, the school instituted a new and more demanding spelling curriculum that year. Where Alia had once worked hard to get A's on her spelling

Computers play a growing role in our world today—but a young person who struggles with a learning disorder may feel as though her disability hampers her from participating in the world of e-mail and Instant Messenger.

Many students with learning disorders also have difficulty getting along with their peers.

dreamed she would do—working as a prostitute and dealing drugs.

CAUSES OF LEARNING DISORDERS

Learning disorders are being studied in depth, and even the experts don't yet have all the answers as to what causes them. However, it is known that there are areas in the human brain that control our behaviors, such as how we process language, how we pay attention and plan, and how we perceive things visually. When these areas have abnormalities, it can result in learning disorders.

When a small area of the brain functions abnormally, this causes a learning disorder. Each of our brains work differ-

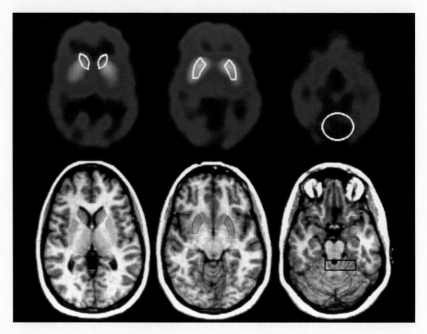

Learning disorders are caused when a small area of the brain does not function normally.

ently from anyone else's, but a learning disorder is a question of degree; when a neurological abnormality interferes with an individual's ability to achieve, particularly in a school setting, then this type of disorder is diagnosed. The disorders may be caused by birth trauma, genetics, or minimal brain damage caused by drugs, either before or after birth. Learning disorders can also be the result of later illnesses and injuries. Encephalitis and meningitis—brain infections—can damage parts of the brain, as can accidents.

Children with these disorders do not lack intelligence; however, they do lack the mental ability to perform specific skills necessary for academic success. Successful learning requires that we first be able to input information. Then we must integrate and understand the information. Next, we must store the information in our memories, and last, we must be able to output information, expressing the information we have learned. Children with a learning disorder have difficulty with one or more of these steps.

You can be surrounded by people—but if you feel
that everyone else is different from you, you might as
well be all alone on a desert island.
—Martin Fuller

4

ANOTHER WORLD

After the night Dad introduced me to Janet, things at home went from bad to worse. Janet started visiting a lot—just about every evening.

Dad tried to act mature and fatherly. "We want to wait as long as it takes for you to be comfortable with Janet before we get married, Charlie," he told me.

But what was the use of waiting, I wondered, when they hardly even noticed I was there? They tried to include me in their conversations at first, but they'd get so involved in whatever they were discussing that they didn't even notice when I slipped out the back door. And Dad had this look on his face all the time now—a look like maybe someone had turned a light bulb on inside him.

Part of me was glad he was so happy. So I said, sure, go ahead, get married as soon as you want. And they did.

The rest of me felt two ways: sad that I wasn't enough to make Dad happy, and mad—really mad—at the person who did make him happy. I dealt with the anger and sadness by getting out of the house as much as I could. Anything to get away from Janet. Even school, as much as I'd always hated it, felt like an escape for once.

We'd never had a school counselor as long as I'd been at Corando, but that year the school system had decided to hire one. It turned out this counselor, Mr. Gordon, was an art teacher, too. We'd never had one of those in Corando, either. Mr. Gordon did his counseling half the day and taught art the other half. The school even set up one of those ugly temporary buildings as an art room, and I have to admit, that became the best place in school for me.

Mr. Gordon didn't talk a lot, but when he did, there was something about him that made you *want* to listen. One day, he spent a long time studying a drawing I'd done, then asked me to stay after class. I was pretty worried about that, since I figure you're always better off to stay away from teachers if you can, but there was no way out of it.

After everybody left, he spread out my drawing on his desk. "You ever thought about cartooning, Charlie?"

I shook my head, which was half way between a lie and the truth. I'd always secretly thought that people who could sit around drawing cartoons for a living were about the luckiest people in the world. On the other hand, I never thought it was something *I* could do. Besides, when I looked at the comics in the Sunday paper at Jake's house, I had to stick to the ones without words.

"I think you could be really good at this kind of drawing," Mr. Gordon said. "Why not develop an idea and plan out a four-panel strip? You could enter it in the Spring Art Fair."

I must have looked crazy, standing there speechless, but no teacher had ever told me I could be "really good" at something. Most of them just seemed sad when they looked at my work.

"Sure," I said finally. "That'd be cool."

I had no clue of what I was getting myself into.

Meanwhile, at home, Janet was driving me crazy.

There hadn't been any books around our house before, except for the ones I had to bring home from school every day and the picture books Dad bought when I was little.

But things changed the minute Janet moved in. First there were the cookbooks. The part of the kitchen counter where Dad used to toss spare change and pay stubs and keys was like a bookshelf now, with about twenty cookbooks all neatly lined up in a row. Don't get me wrong—Janet's cooking was decent, and we started eating a lot of new things I liked—but why would it take a person twenty books to figure out how to do that?

Janet had boxes and boxes of novels, too—so many that Dad had to build shelves on one wall of the extra bedroom to hold them. One time she told me that reading was the thing that relaxed her the most when she came home from work. I knew right then that we could never be friends. I'd do my best to be polite, but she lived in that *other* world, the one where people with brains like mine couldn't go.

Then she did something else that really bugged me—she put a magazine rack in the *bathroom.* That was just plain wrong. Now I felt like books were surrounding me on every side, squeezing me in somehow.

The night after that talk with Mr. Gordon, I told my dad the news about the comic strip. A few days later, I noticed she put the color comics from the Sunday paper in the bathroom magazine rack. I couldn't help looking at them, and I even got some ideas for my own comic strip drawings. After that, the comics started showing up at our house every week, and that bugged me. I hadn't even been talking to her.

One afternoon, when I got home from school, I grabbed the mail out of the mailbox like I did every night. I usually just carried it inside and tossed it on the kitchen table. But this time there was a magazine on top, and on the cover was a shot of a skier, sailing through the air in the middle of an amazing jump. Behind him you could see range after range of mountain peaks against a brilliant blue sky. I stared at that cover for a long time, feeling that bright sun and the freezing air on my cheeks, hearing the wind whistle past my ears as I jumped with him . . .

"Charlie!"

I really did jump then and dropped the mail. Jake stood beside me, laughing. "Where were you? I called you about twenty times and you never even heard me."

He picked up the mail and straightened it out. When he got to the magazine, he stopped. "Hey, when'd you subscribe to *Skiing*?"

"I didn't."

"Well, it's got your name on it. See?" He held it under my nose and pointed to the label.

It had to be Janet's doing, of course. She just smiled at me when I questioned her, and said my dad had told her once that I wanted to ski someday. I was mad at her for trying to push her way into my life, but in my room later that night, I couldn't resist leafing through that magazine. The pictures looked so real you could feel the snow underneath you and imagine how it'd be to race down those slopes. There were snowboarders in those pictures, too. I'd never really thought about snowboarding before—but I did now. And I wanted to know more about it. There were all these words under the pictures that could tell me, but it took me so long to sound them out that I couldn't remember what the words at the beginning of the caption said by the time I got to those at the end. I made Jake read them to me, but every time a new magazine came in the mail, the frustration started all over again.

That was bad enough—Janet butting her nose into my business that way, Janet spreading books all over the house—but then she went too far. One night, the three of us were finishing up a lasagna dinner. Janet's lasagna is good enough that even I like her better on the night she makes it, so I was feeling pretty good until Dad said he had news.

"You'll never believe what Janet's going to do, Charlie," he said, mopping up the last of the cheesy tomato sauce with a piece of bread. He looked as proud as when they gave him a new delivery truck at work last year.

Probably not, I thought, but I've learned not to say that kind of thing out loud.

"She's going to teach me to read, son, something I've always wanted to do." He paused, waiting for me to tell him how great that was, so I did. Then he went on. "So I was wondering if you'd look up in the attic and find those picture books for me, the ones you used to read to me, remember?"

My heart started to race. Once he learned to read—really read—he'd know that I'd been faking it when I "read" those books to him.

MEMORY DISORDERS

"Memory is a complicated multidepartmental operation that does its work at many diverse brain sites, a lot of which have not even been located by neuroscientists. Nothing is ever learned without tapping into some component of memory."
—Dr. Mel Levine, *A Mind at a Time*

Short-term memory is the first stop for the information that is constantly bombarding our minds, and the capacity of that stop is extremely limited. Most adults can retain only seven numbers at a time in their short-term memory, and children can manage only four or five numbers. Within a time span of less than two seconds, however, we have to decide whether to let the information go or to hold on to it by storing it in our long-term memory. Students, especially, deal with this task throughout an average school day.

Some students have problems getting the information into their long-term memory, and this can be yet another learning difficulty. Some students can easily grab and hold on to certain types of information, yet quickly lose other types. Certain students may need to have information presented to them very slowly in order to adequately grasp and hold on to it.

Memory strategies, such as summarizing, paraphrasing, and visualizing, can be used to help students with memory disorders. *A Mind at a Time* provides helpful information on this subject.

LINKED DISORDERS

"Three common learning disorders, one common bond," writes B. Jacqueline Stordy, Ph.D., in *The LCP Solution; the Remarkable Nutritional Treatment for ADHD, Dyslexia, &*

A student who struggles with a learning disorder may also face a psychiatric disorder like ADHD, bipolar disorder, or Tourette's syndrome.

Dyspraxia. "There is no doubt that ADHD, dyslexia, and dyspraxia run in families. (For more information on dyspraxia, see page 81.) There is no doubt that some children are afflicted with two—sometimes even all three—of these [conditions]. It is time that health and education professionals recognized the interrelationship so that the most effective treatments can be introduced in the earliest years of these children's lives."

Stordy writes that up to 65 percent of children who have ADHD also have at least one other learning disorder. They may also have **bipolar disorder** and/or **Tourette's syndrome**.

In a study of more than 400 seven-year-old children, it was found that 50 percent of those who have dyspraxia also have ADHD. From 30 to 50 percent of children with dyslexia have ADHD. The reverse is also true. Some researchers, such as those at the Dyslexia Research Institute, have found that statistic to be even higher and maintain that 60 percent of children with ADHD also have dyslexia.

THE STEPS TO LEARNING

1. input
2. integration
3. memory
4. output

Input

if a child cannot correctly perceive written shapes, then he will not be able to input the information contained in

A child with a learning disorder may have difficulty perceiving written shapes.

The ability to put things in a sequence is a vital skill for understanding mathematics.

writing. Reading requires that our eyes focus on specific letters or groups of letters and then track from left to right, line after line. Children with a reading disorder, however, may skip over words, read the same line twice, or skip lines. They may not be able to distinguish the shapes of letters, or they may not be able to focus on the letters as opposed to the white spaces around them. This does not mean that there is anything wrong with their eyes; it simply means that their brains have difficulty inputting written information.

Integration

If a child has trouble with the integration step of the learning process, then she may not be able to sequence, abstract, or organize. These skills are necessary components of doing mathematics; they are also important parts of making sense out of a story—or writing a paragraph. Children who cannot sequence easily may have trouble learning to count or learning the alphabet; they may have a hard time learning the days of the week or the months of the year. If a child has difficulty making abstractions, then he is only able to deal with things from a completely literal point of view. He may not be able to apply what he has learned to a new situation; he can only view facts in the exact situation in which they were first presented, rather than being able to make generalizations. And a child who cannot organize information will not be able to put together what she has learned into one picture.

Memory

Children who have a problem with the memory step of learning will obviously be unable to perform well on tests. However, if their short-term memory is so poor that they cannot remember what they have read from one paragraph to the next, or what the teacher said five minutes ago, their learning will be impaired at an even more basic level.

Output

A child who has difficulty with the output level of learning may have a writing disorder. He may also have a communication or motor-skills disorder. These disorders often accompany learning disorders.

POSSIBLE SIGNS OF DYSLEXIA IN YOUNG ADULTS AND ADULTS

The problems listed on page 74 may indicate dyslexia if they are unexpected, given an individual's age, level of

A learning disorder does not mean a person cannot complete high school and attend college!

education, and cognitive abilities. Only a qualified diagnostician, however, can determine if a person is dyslexic.

High School and College-Aged Students

- Reads slowly, with frequent inaccuracies.
- Has an ongoing problem with spelling (even spelling the same word different ways within one piece of writing).
- Avoids reading and writing if at all possible.
- Has difficulty summarizing.
- Has poor memory skills.
- Works slowly.
- Exhibits inappropriate attention to details—either too little or too much.
- Has an inadequate vocabulary.
- Exhibits difficulty in planning, organizing, and managing of time, materials, and tasks.

A college or high school student with a reading disorder is apt to avoid reading out loud in class.

Adults

- Hides his or her problems with reading.
- Spells poorly and depends on other people to correct spelling.
- Avoids writing.
- Relies on memory.
- Exhibits good "people" skills; is intuitive and able to "read" other people.
- Frequently is spatially talented.
- May be working in a job that requires far less intellectual capacity than he or she has.

There are offenses given and offenses
not given but taken.
—Izaak Walton

5

CONFLICTS

I decided I had to get rid of those picture books—and fast—and because I hung around with Jake, who loved the public library, I knew the perfect place to dump them.

As soon as Dad and Janet left for work the next morning, I rummaged around in the attic till I found them. Then, the minute I got home from school, I lugged the whole box down to the library. It has a sign just inside the back door that Jake told me says "Book Sale Books"; it has an arrow pointing to the floor. People leave lots of books beneath that sign, and there's always at least one box of old *National Geographic*s.

Just as I set my box down, the librarian came out to collect the donations.

"You're just in time for the sale this Saturday," she told me. When she carried off my box, I felt relieved that Dad wouldn't discover my secret, but bad because I knew I'd have to lie.

At dinner, Dad asked me, "Did you look for those books, Charlie?"

I nodded, my mouth full of broiled pork chop.

"So, where are they?"

"Well, I—I'm not really sure where they are, Dad," I told him. And technically, that was the truth. I had no idea where the librarian had put my box.

"Oh." His face was disappointed, which made me feel worse than ever. "You didn't find them?"

I took an extra-long time chewing the green beans. "Uh, they don't seem to be anywhere in the house." *That* was certainly true, too, up to a point.

Janet gave me this long look she has that makes me wriggle around in my chair a little. I'm always worried that if she looks at me that way long enough, she'll see right through me. "Don't worry, Honey," she told my dad, "I'll find other books we can use."

But later that evening, something happened that made me think that Janet suspected something. She walked into the kitchen where I was packing my lunch for the next day.

"So, Charlie," she said, measuring coffee grounds into the paper filter as she spoke, "how'd you like that last skiing magazine?"

"It's great. Thanks."

"How about that article on ski resorts in the Rockies?"

"I liked it a lot," I lied.

"Oh, good. Tell me, if you could visit any one of those resorts, which one would it be?"

She had me then. I took a wild guess. "Purgatory," I told her, hoping with all my might that Purgatory had been one of the resorts.

"Hmmm, I didn't see Purgatory in that article." I started thinking of some way to cover up my blunder, but she went right on. "I've always liked Purgatory, though."

I stared at her. "You *ski*?"

Janet smiled at me. "Sure. I grew up in Durango, and my high school had a ski club. We used to go every Monday night."

"How long would it take for somebody to learn to ski? A beginner, say?" I tore a banana off the bunch on the counter and stuck it in my lunch bag, trying to act nonchalant.

"The way *you* skateboard? You'd be sailing down those slopes in half an hour, Charlie."

I could hardly look at her, I felt so proud when she said that.

The picture of myself on skis suddenly looked very much within reach. Then I remembered something, and the picture shattered.

"Dad says skiing's too expensive for us."

Janet laughed out loud. "Tell you what, Charlie. If you'll help me with something, I think I can change his mind. There are two of us earning money here now, remember?"

My heart was in my throat. "What d'you want me to do?"

"I'd like you to help me teach your dad to read."

I turned away from her, biting my lip. "Oh. I thought you meant something like cleaning out the garage," I said, and leaned into the fridge to put my lunch away so she couldn't see my face. "I probably wouldn't have time to help with Dad."

Janet set the timer on the coffeemaker. "That's too bad, Charlie. He'd learn much quicker if we both helped. Sure you couldn't spare just an hour or two a week?"

"I'm awful busy with homework. Thanks, though," I said. "Listen, I'm going to my room now. Jake's coming over so we can work on stuff for school."

I was halfway out the kitchen doorway when Janet called after me, "Charlie, if you change your mind, my offer will still be good."

Things came to a head between us not long after that.

Jake and I kept right on working on homework together every day, like usual. Then one afternoon, when I was sitting on the kitchen counter eating cupcakes and listening to Jake read our history assignment out loud, Janet walked in, two hours earlier than she ever had before.

I don't think she would've suspected anything if Jake didn't act so guilty. He had both our homework papers laid out in front of him on the kitchen table, using a blue pen for one and a black one for the other, the way he always did. When Janet walked in, he whipped those papers under the history book so fast he looked downright criminal.

Janet stared at him, her head tilted to one side. She glanced at me, then back at Jake. "I thought you were *both* doing homework," she commented.

I guess guilt puts you on the defensive, because I shot right back, "And I thought you and Dad were *both* working," in my most disrespectful tone of voice.

Janet held out her hand toward Jake. "May I see those papers?"

Jake looked almost as scared as I felt. What if she started putting it all together—my mistake about the skiing article, my refusal to help Dad learn to read, and now this?

I slid off the counter and got between her and Jake. "No," I said. "You don't need to see them. They're just history homework, and we don't need supervision."

Janet kept her hand out and laughed a little, as though to lighten things up. "You know how parents are."

"No," I shot back, "I don't. My dad never bothers me about my homework. And *you're* not my parent." I wished I could take back the words as soon as I saw the look on her face, but it was too late.

MOTOR-SKILLS DISORDER

This disorder seldom occurs alone; it almost always accompanies a learning disorder or some other psychiatric disorder. Children with this disorder are clumsy; they have trouble coordinating their muscle movements. According to the American Psychiatric Press, about five percent of all children have significant fine motor or **gross motor skills**. Since athletic ability is valued highly in our culture, children with this disorder may suffer from poor self-esteem. They will dread gym class and seek to avoid any physical activity that would make them demonstrate their lack of physical grace.

Dyspraxia

Dyspraxia, which involves problems with planning and execution of movements, often results in a child appearing awkward, clumsy, and uncoordinated.

Motor weaknesses figure largely in social acceptance and self-image. The inability to play sports, for instance, can lead to the painful, but common, playground situation in which a certain child is invariably the last to be chosen for a team. Usually, such a child has no idea why he can't catch a softball dependably or sink a basketball accurately, and simply decides that he is "stupid" or "dumb." Dr. Mel Levine sums up the situation this way: "Humiliating performance in sports deflates self-esteem the way a sharp nail in your driveway leads to a flat tire, especially in a kid whose report card also leaves a whole lot to be desired."

Graphomotor Function

Graphomotor function is one area where motor weakness can cause extreme difficulty for young students. This painful inability to form letters fluently on paper often leaves

Children with learning disabilities may be teased by other students.

students all too ready to avoid writing in any form, and since so much of school involves writing, to avoid school also. Children who cannot write find themselves being teased by other students, especially when students grade one another's papers. They often cannot complete tests within a given time frame and find written homework extraordinarily tiring.

LABELING—A DANGEROUS BUSINESS

Dr. Mel Levine, a widely recognized expert on learning differences and the author of *A Mind at a Time*, explains that labeling can dehumanize a person and even consume a person's identity. He adds that it can be frightening to hear a person say something like, "I am ADD." To underscore the impact of such a statement, he asks, "Can you imagine someone proclaiming, 'I am bronchial asthma?'"

Labeling, writes Dr. Levine, is "reductionistic. It oversimplifies kids," and "overlooks their richness, their complexity, their strengths, and their striking originality."

Labeling can also imply that a present problem may be lifelong, though Levine denies that there is evidence for this. Instead, he comments that such an implication "denies the resiliency we know drives the human central nervous system." (From *A Mind at a Time*, by Mel Levine, M.D., p. 328.)

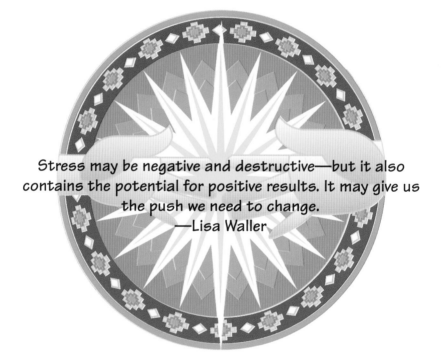

Stress may be negative and destructive—but it also contains the potential for positive results. It may give us the push we need to change.
—Lisa Waller

6

TENSIONS

Things were tense at my house after that day, but Janet was smart enough not to tell my dad what had happened.

I felt uneasy, though, almost like we were playing some weird kind of cat-and-mouse game. Unfortunately, I was the mouse and she was watching me.

Nearly every night Janet and Dad sat at the kitchen table after dinner, books spread out in front of them. Patiently, Janet went over and over the sounds the different letters make. Within a couple of days, Dad was starting to read all those little first-grade words—cat, mat, hat—that kind of stuff.

Even I know those words, so now and then I'd lean over Dad's shoulder and read a couple to him, tell him he was doing a great job, and then get out of the kitchen as quick as I could. But I could still feel Janet watching. A couple times she asked me to stay and help, but I always made some excuse.

Then she got trickier. "Charlie," she called as I rushed through the kitchen on the way to my bedroom one evening, "I'm busy getting dinner here, so could you look through the mail on the table and figure out what's important and what goes into the trash?"

I tossed all the dress catalogs and flyers from local stores into the trash—anybody can tell they aren't important—but when I got to the letters, it was a different story. "Here," I told her, "I'll leave these on the table for you to look at later."

SPATIAL OR SEQUENCING DIFFICULTIES

Our minds commonly use two ordering systems to help us function in this world:

1. The spatial system, which is usually centered in the right side of the brain and helps us perceive spatial patterns, such as the features of another person's face.
2. The sequential system, which is usually centered in the left side of the brain and helps us process information that must be kept in a particular order, such as the months of the year and telephone numbers.

Our brains' ability to create a sequential system allows us to perform activities that must be done in a particular order.

Computer programs can provide opportunities for children with learning disorders to practice sequencing activities.

For students with learning problems in these areas, learning experiences that most of us take for granted can be extremely difficult or, at best, frustrating. These students may find it nearly impossible to learn the days of the week, the sequential steps in a long division problem, or even the letters of the alphabet.

Sequencing difficulties affect more than just classroom activities. A child with such problems may dress himself without any regard for sequential order. Or he may find it almost impossible to relate experiences to another person in sequential order. Time management problems also fall into this category, as do problems with the concepts behind words such as *before* and *after*.

A special education teacher may work individually with a student to help him manage his school schedule and assigned homework projects.

Dr. Mel Levine suggests these and other steps to help children with spatial and sequential challenges:

- Students should wear analog rather than digital watches.
- Schools should stress time management, directing students to come up with schedules and to accomplish their projects in stages, showing each stage of their work while it is under way.
- Parents can use rhythmic games and songs to reinforce sequential ordering with young children. The alphabet song, and songs about the months of the year or days of the week, are good examples.
- Parents can also help with spatial ordering by providing children with an organized area at home in which to do their homework.

I am not the smartest or most talented person . . . but I
succeeded because I keep going, and going, and going.
—Sylvester Stallone

7

THE POWER
OF PERSISTENCE

When Janet got home from work that night, I was waiting for her.

"You talked to Mr. Gordon about me?" I demanded, even before she got the door closed behind her.

Janet took a deep breath, as though she'd been expecting this conversation, then nodded as she starting taking off her coat. "Somebody had to do something, Charlie."

"What are you *talking* about? I'm doing just fine. I have everything worked out! What makes you think you have the right to stick your nose into my business, anyway?"

Janet hung her coat in the hall closet, then turned to face me, speaking deliberately. "In one sense, I guess I don't, Charlie, since I'm not technically your parent. You seem to like Mr. Gordon, and I thought perhaps he'd be the best one to talk to you about your reading problems. So I took a chance and told him, because I believe that caring a lot about someone gives you the right to do what's best for them."

She walked toward the kitchen and started pulling things out of the freezer for dinner. I followed her, fuming.

"And what exactly did you tell Mr. Gordon while you were doing what was 'best' for me?" I put as much sarcasm as I could into my words, but she started slicing celery as though she hadn't even noticed.

"I told him the truth—that you can't read well enough to get by."

"Are you *crazy*?" I shouted. "How do you think I made it to seventh grade?"

"Probably the same way I did." She scraped the celery slices into the skillet and started chopping an onion.

"What'd you say?"

"I said that you probably did it the same way I did—you just keep getting passed from grade to grade because the teachers don't really know what to do with you. And you think up lots of creative ways to get your homework done. I didn't have a friend like Jake, though, so I was a lot better off than you."

"You don't like Jake?"

Janet laughed. "I like Jake very much. I just don't think that having him around to do your homework is helping you in the long run."

"What are you talking about, 'do my homework'?"

Janet looked up from the onion long enough to roll her eyes at me. "You really do think adults are blind, don't you? Well, you may have fooled your dad—though he has a better of idea of what's going on than you may think—but don't think you're going to fool me. I go to the library, too, you know. And the librarian couldn't wait to tell me about that whole box of books you donated. It wasn't hard to figure out what was going on after that."

I stared at Janet, my mouth open. I thought I'd fooled everyone, but she had me all figured out. I knew she must think I was a terrible liar now, and I wanted to slink away. At the same time, I wanted to yell at her and tell her to stay out of my business—out of my *life*, actually. But I did neither of those things. In the end, my curiosity got the better of me.

"What did you mean before, when you said I probably made it to seventh grade the same way you did?"

Janet scraped the onions into the skillet with the celery, then washed her hands. "Sit down here at the table and I'll tell you."

The story she told me sounded kind of familiar.

"My parents had big dreams for me, Charlie. Kind of like your dad has for you, I think. My folks never even graduated from high school, and they were determined that I was going to be the first one in the family to do that. So you can imagine how they felt when the school decided I should be held back at the end of second grade, Charlie."

Janet got up and went to the stove, stirred the sizzling celery and onions, then added ground beef to the pan. "The only thing the teacher told me was that I couldn't do arithmetic as well as the other kids and that people like me couldn't do very well in the third grade, so I'd have to try second grade again. There was no offer of special help, no recognition of my other strengths—I was one of the best readers in the class—just this feeling that I was being punished for something I had no control over. And when I got held back, the other kids all decided I must be really dumb, no matter how well I could read."

I squirmed a little in my seat, thinking of all the times I'd heard that word in the last few years.

"My parents never really got any answers from my school. The fact that they were Navajo and Hispanic, and not highly educated themselves—all that counted pretty heavily against them. And repeating second grade seemed to set a pattern for the rest of my years at school. It's not a time I like to look back on."

"But you said you had a ski club and that you went skiing with them every week and . . ."

Janet replaced the lid on the skillet and sat down across the table from me again. "You're right, I did, and it helped keep me from losing my mind. If it hadn't been for ski club, I probably would've dropped out of school even sooner."

I think my mouth must have fallen open at that point, because Janet laughed out loud when she looked at me.

"*You* dropped out?" I said.

She nodded. "Sure. Lots of kids do when they face the kind of problems I did. I knew I was smart in some areas—I loved to read by then, for instance. And I was good in phys. ed. and was even faster than any of the boys. But I got no encouragement because I was just seen as the 'dumb kid,' and I knew I could never pass the higher level courses. Do you have any idea how much math there is in the college prep course? A distant cousin of my father's had moved away from this area, gone to college, and started a business of his own in Dallas. He offered me a job in sales—said he'd teach me what I needed to know himself. So I dropped out of school and went to work for him. If I had had a mentor—or even another student who would admit to having the same problem—I might have stuck it out. But I just assumed I was the only one in the world with this problem."

By then, I'd forgotten how angry I was at her. "But you do math now. I've seen you balancing your checkbook. What happened?"

"Something pretty great, actually. While I was working in Dallas, I heard about a woman there who ran a school for kids with severe learning disabilities. The local TV channel did some human interest stories on her and featured some of the students she'd helped. By that time, I was already in my mid-twenties, so I knew I could never be in her school. But I also knew that I didn't want to go through the rest of my life without even getting my high school diploma. So I called her up and asked if she knew how to help people my age."

"And?"

"And it turned out she tutored adults after school nearly every day, adults who were just like me. So she did some testing and told me I had something called dyscalculia. I started working with her a couple of times a week, for about three years, and I found out that even someone like me can learn to do math—given the right kind of help and a whole lot of stick-to-itiveness!"

"A lot of *what?*"

"Persistence. Lots and lots of persistence." She folded her hands on the table between us and looked at me, hard. "Something I think you have, Charlie Begay, along with a real talent in art, maybe even with numbers. I don't want you to drop out of school and end up getting a **GED** the way I did, or thinking that you're dumb. I was in my mid-twenties before I found out why I couldn't cope with math. From what I found out about learning disorders back then, I really think you may be struggling with dyslexia. And I think that may be the same reason your dad could never learn to read when he was in school. Sometimes, these things run in families."

In bed that night, I thought about what Janet told me. Our stories were so different, yet so similar. And I couldn't help thinking about the nice things she had said about me, too.

Maybe—just maybe—having Janet around might not be all that bad.

HIGHER ORDER THINKING DEFICIENCIES

The mind's highest abilities enable us to understand and process concepts, which are ideas or thoughts that are sometimes abstract, complex, or difficult to follow. When students study history, for example, they have to wrestle with the meanings of "democracy" or "dictatorship." In science, they must understand processes such as "photosynthesis" and "respiration." If a student's learning disorder is a deficiency in this higher order of thinking, classes that require such thinking become difficult, even intimidating.

Other learning disorders in this category may make it difficult for students to understand math or grammar rules, or to use problem-solving skills.

A student with a learning disorder may find it difficult to respond appropriately in class.

A special education teacher can help students develop strategies to compensate for their difficulties.

Strategies That Help

Healthcare and education professionals recommend that classroom strategies be developed to accommodate the special needs of students with learning disorders. Examples of such strategies might include:

- allowing a student with dysgraphia to take a test orally, or assigning him to complete half of a homework assignment in writing and half orally.
- giving a student with attention deficit extra time to complete a test or assignment.
- allowing the use of word processors for students with writing difficulties.
- allowing the use of handheld recorders for those with writing and memory difficulties.
- providing a copy of class notes for students whose learning disorder makes notetaking difficult.

For a person with a learning disability, a stack of books may seem like a mountain that is impossible to scale.

Some educators excel at developing strategies that minimize their students' disabilities and maximize their strengths. One teacher devised an arrangement about spelling tests with a student who had dysgraphia. This student was reluctant to appear different from her classmates in any way and so she would take each spelling test along with her class. Later, however, she was free to go to the teacher in private, usually during lunch or recess, and spell the words orally. The teacher took into account only the words the student spelled to her in private.

A student with a pronounced weakness expressing himself verbally lived in dread of being called on in class. The teacher agreed to give him a warning that he would be called on in certain classes, and to allow him more time than usual to verbalize his thoughts.

Teachers may choose to maximize the strengths of their students with learning disorders by designing ways for them to excel in their particular areas of strength. This may include allowing an artistic student to help design stage sets for school plays or musicals; or allowing a student who is talented with computers to help tutor others who are not yet "computer literate."

One of the best strategies for students with learning disorders that affect their writing and notetaking abilities is to learn to use a keyboard. Becoming a proficient typist can help a student feel that he or she has been "set free" from the confines of being unable to write.

An exciting method for dealing with dyslexia is called the Wilson Reading System, first published in 1988, which is an extension of the Orton-Gillingham method. The system was developed by Barbara Wilson, who taught students with dyslexia at Massachusetts General Hospital from 1983 to 1988. The Wilson system enables students to master the "coding system" for both reading and spelling, and teaches

With the proper educational support, many students with learning disabilities can succeed.

students how to "pull sounds apart in a given word or syllable."

Students learn crucial skills, such as **segmentation**, which involves breaking words into both syllable segments and **phonemene** (the smallest measure of sound) segments. The system uses five main principles:

- knowing the alphabetic code.
- knowing how to analyze language, which includes knowing prefixes, suffixes, **digraphs**, **diphthongs**, and the system English uses to **syllabify**.
- learning reading and spelling simultaneously.
- intensive reading instruction, including a great deal of practicing.
- teaching for **automaticity**.
  (From http://userpages.acadia.net/waldolva/ wilson/wilson.html. Much more detailed information on the Wilson Reading System is available at this site.)

Nothing can be done without hope or confidence.
—Helen Keller

8

HOPE

Funny how I'd been so furious with Janet just a little while before and then felt entirely different after we talked. Sometimes when you find out what another person's been through, you start thinking differently about why they do things.

Instead of being furious that Janet was "interfering" in my life, I could now see that she wanted to keep me from experiencing some of the tough times she'd gone through. And somewhere, in the back of my mind, this idea started up that maybe I wasn't just a loser. If I had dyslexia—the way Janet had dyscalculia—maybe I could over-come it the same as she did. *Maybe.*

First, there was a lot of stuff that had to change. Janet lined up some tests at a special clinic in Albuquerque. I had to meet with Dr. Baxter there, who knew a lot about learning disorders, especially dyslexia. The tests he gave me weren't really hard or anything, but there were a lot of questions I needed to answer, so the tests took two days. There were physical tests, too, like a long eye exam to make sure my eyes were working okay and that I didn't need glasses.

Janet and my dad both took time off from work so the three of us could go together. After the second day of testing, Janet said I de-served some kind of reward for being such a good patient, and they took me to this place outside the city, Sandia Peak, where we rode the tramway. The sign said it was the longest aerial tramway in the world. You can't believe the view we saw from up there—miles and miles of New Mexico, spread out all around. And then we drove

105

around to the area for beginning skiers, and Janet gave me and Dad our first ski lesson. I think that my dad on the bunny hill would've made a terrific comedy movie, but by the end of the evening, both of us could make it down the hill without any trouble at all.

When we went back to Albuquerque the following week for the test results, Dr. Baxter said I definitely had dyslexia. He sat on the edge of his desk and talked to me more than he did to Janet and my dad, and that made me feel good, like I mattered. He said I had a really high *IQ*, which stands for intelligence quotient, and that someday I was going to be able to follow my own interests and do really well at them if I just didn't give up on school. He also said I needed to work with the kind of tutor Janet had had and that I could learn to read with some specialized help.

Then he made sure I got a chance to ask any questions I had, so I asked him about the letters moving around on the page back when I was in first grade.

"That's actually one of the symptoms of dyslexia, Charlie," he told me. "Not a lot of people have that one, but I've heard of it a couple of times now."

I think that's when I started to really believe that I might not be totally weird and began to look forward to learning to read. When he recommended a tutor he knew, who used something called the Wilson Reading System and lived in a little town about half an hour from my house, I was actually excited about the idea.

"It would be ideal if you could have gotten the help you needed earlier, Charlie," he told me, "but since that hasn't worked, we need to do whatever we can to help you now."

After that, there were meetings with the teacher and principal and Mr. Gordon, and they drew up a plan just for me. Janet explained to them, pleasantly but firmly, that the tutors I had had up to that time had not helped me learn to read. Because of her, they agreed to take Dr. Baxter's suggestion and let me study with Ron Cianno, the tutor who uses Wilson. I meet with him during the time I used to go to study hall.

At first, I felt like working on the dyslexia was a mountain too huge to climb—like I'd never be able to overcome it. But little by little, Ron helped me understand things about how the English language is put together and ways I could remember which letters made which sounds.

The Wilson Reading System teaches you things like digraphs and welded sounds and the rules of syllable division—and a whole bunch more things than I can ever fit here. Gradually, you start to see patterns in the words on the page in front of you. One of the first things I learned was the vowel drill, which helped me remember the different sounds vowels can make. Ron also taught me how to tap out words using my fingers and thumb.

There are some things we do at every tutoring session—sight words and my magnetic journal, for instance, where Ron dictates and I use magnetic letters to spell out whatever he says on the side panels of the journal. Sometimes he just dictates sounds, like "sh" and "k"—Did you know there are three different ways to spell the "k" sound? Ron says it's no wonder English confuses people. When he says those kinds of things, I don't feel dumb anymore.

Naturally, we always read. Ron worked hard to find out what I was interested in, and after our first couple of sessions, he always had a book or magazine on skateboarding, snowboarding, or skiing ready for me. And when I did my best, he rewarded me with some of the greatest posters you've ever seen. My walls are still plastered with those posters.

After about a year of working with Ron, I was reading well enough that Jake and I had to come to an understanding.

"Look, Jake," I told him one afternoon when we finished studying for history, "I don't know if you're getting the idea here or not, but I have to stop paying you for the homework. I mean, I'm doing almost all of it myself now, but I didn't want to make you feel unneeded, you know?"

Jake turned around from the cupcake drawer. "You telling me you think you can do this stuff by yourself?"

I shrugged. "Well—yeah!"

"Like, totally on your own? And still pass?"

This was getting harder than I'd planned. "Of course. Can't you see how much things have changed this year?" I launched into this big explanation of how I could read so much better and how much I'd learned, until Jake broke in, grinning.

"Well, I was wondering when you were gonna say so, man," he said.

I stared at him for a second. "What?"

He laughed out loud and punched me in the shoulder. "Hey, I've just been stealing your money these past couple months. I wondered when you were gonna wise up."

I put him in a headlock then, until he swore he'd pay back every cent from the last couple of months.

"Okay, already, I'll pay you back." He finally squirmed his way out of my hold. "But just remember," he said, as soon as he was free, "you'll still never read as well as me!"

I took out after him then, yelling, "Oh, yeah? So maybe we better find you a skateboard tutor, 'cuz you'll *never* board the way I do!"

Later, when we were through goofing off, Jake asked me if I thought Janet could get him some help with his math, and I promised I'd talk to her about it.

I couldn't believe how great it felt to finally be learning to read, but in the spring of that year, another good thing happened. My cartoon took third place in the Spring Art Fair. To make it even better, the *Corando Weekly* paid me twenty-five dollars to print it. Suddenly, some of the kids who had been calling me "dumb" for years started treating me different. One even asked me to sign her copy of the *Weekly*.

Jake had lots of ideas about how I should spend that money, but I had something special I wanted to do with it. I went back to the public library and asked the librarian if any picture books were left from last year's book sale. She let me in the room where they stored the books for the next annual sale, and I found two of the books Dad had given me years ago. I bought them back, and that night after dinner I showed them to my father and explained why I'd gotten rid of them in the first place.

"I'm sorry, Dad," I told him. "I should've just been straight with you instead of lying. But I'd like you to have these back now, and maybe sometime I can read you what they really say."

I should have known he would understand. All he said was, "Or I can read them to you, the way I always wished I could when you were little!"

INDIVIDUALIZED EDUCATION PLAN (IEP)

An IEP is a written plan designed specifically for each special education child. It defines reasonable expectations for achievement and how success will be determined. It should include these points:

1. A statement of the child's current level of education performance.
2. A statement of yearly goals or achievements expected for each area of identified weakness by the end of the school year.
3. Short-term objectives stated in instructional terms (concrete, observable steps leading to the mastery of the yearly goals).

In each class, no two students are alike. An IEP ensures that each student with special needs will have an educational plan that matches her unique needs.

Many students in special education programs can also participate in "regular" classes.

4. A statement of the specific special education and support services to be provided to the child.
5. A statement of the extent to which a child will be able to participate in regular education programs and justification for any special placement recommended.
6. Projected dates for the beginning of services and how long they are anticipated to last.
7. A statement of the criteria and evaluation procedures to be used in determining (on at least an annual basis, if not more frequently) whether the short-term objectives have been achieved.

Students with learning disorders will achieve more when they have a healthy respect for their own value as individuals.

WHAT DO STUDENTS NEED MOST?

In one of the stories on the Schwab Learning Web site, Dr. Jodie Dawson interviews a young man who grew up hiding his learning disorder until he gave a speech about it at his high school graduation. When Dr. Dawson asked what would have helped him most when he was younger, he said:

- having other kids his age to talk to about his learning disorder.
- having a mentor who had also grown up with a learning disorder.
- educating other people about his condition; correcting misinformation.
- learning to advocate for himself. (As an example, he cited feeling unintelligent because he was placed in the low reading group in his class. Because there was no moving between the low and high reading

All young people need kids their own age with whom they can socialize, learn, and have fun.

groups, he had to practice **self-advocacy** for two years before he could move up.)

SUFFERING IN SILENCE

Students with learning disorders often struggle and suffer in private to overcome their problems on their own, sometimes because they are too ashamed to ask for help (believing that they are "dumb" and just need to work harder), and sometimes because they don't know whom to ask.

For example, Shellie grew up with dyslexia. In her case, this meant that she not only read at about half the speed that other people did but also remembered only about half of what she read. Her "strategy" was to work at her homework from the time she got home from school until very late at night, sometimes even getting out of bed to go back to work on undone assignments after she was sure her parents were in bed and asleep. The only way she knew to overcome her problem was to memorize every word of her study sheets and notes—most of which she never actually needed again—in the hope that she would not miss any information she might need for a test or quiz.

Adam had dysgraphia, but did not know his learning disorder by that name for several years. All he heard from others was that he "wrote like a baby!" and couldn't even "color in the lines!" Classmates in his third- and fourth-grade classes regularly made fun of his writing, especially when students exchanged papers for grading. Heidi and Amber, especially, felt it was their duty to remind him at least once each day that no one on *earth* could read his writing—and in fact, probably no one in the *entire universe* could.

When he started failing spelling tests because the teacher could no longer decipher his writing, Adam's parents tried to convince him to take his teacher up on her offer to let him spell his words orally. "No!" Adam protested.

"Don't you see? If I do that, then everybody'll know how stupid I am. I have to take my test right along with everybody else!"

In sixth grade, when a kind and understanding expert in learning disorders explained to Adam that he had dysgraphia and listed all the symptoms, Adam broke down and cried. "You mean I'm *not* just stupid?"

A young person with a learning disorder may mistakenly believe she is stupid.

Although students with learning disorders often become discouraged, they can go on to lead successful lives in the world outside school.

DOES HAVING DYSLEXIA MEAN I CANNOT LIVE A SUCCESSFUL LIFE?

Many people with dyslexia go on to lead successful lives. Because so many are spatially talented, it is not uncommon for them to become engineers, architects, designers, and artists. They also frequently work in the fields of mathematics, physics, and medicine, particularly surgery and orthopedics.

It is important that dyslexia be recognized and dealt with appropriately, and that children with this condition receive support from family, teachers, and friends. With this help, many people with dyslexia have made significant contributions to society. Here are just a few examples of people who have done so:

- Charles R. Schwab, the famous discount brokerage pioneer, faced a lifelong struggle with dyslexia. As so often happens, the disorder was passed along to his son. Schwab and his wife, Helen O'Neill Schwab, started the Schwab Foundation for Learning as a result of their efforts to help their own son and others like him. The staff of the foundation, who can be contacted at www.schwablearning.org, will respond personally to questions.
- Ann Bancroft was the first woman to cross the ice to both the North and South Poles.
- David Boies, a trial lawyer, has represented many famous clients, including Napster, the U.S. Justice Department (against Microsoft), and former U.S. Vice President Al Gore.
- Erin Brockovitch, who discovered and helped prosecute a utility company in California that contaminated the local water supply and exposed citizens to potentially deadly health consequences. Because of her actions, the citizens involved were

awarded a settlement of $333 million dollars. Her story was then made into a movie.

- Stephen J. Cannell, an author, TV producer, and writer. He has been involved in the creation of nearly forty shows, including *The Rockford Files*, *A-Team*, *21 Jump Street*, and *Renegade*, and has been awarded an Emmy.

Other People with Learning Disorders Who Have Gone on to Success

Hans Christian Anderson
Harry Belafonte
Alexander Graham Bell
George Burns
Cher
Winston Churchill
Leonardo da Vinci
Walt Disney
Thomas Edison

Albert Einstein
Henry Ford
Danny Glover
Whoopi Goldberg
Jay Leno
General George Patton
Nelson Rockefeller
Woodrow Wilson
W. B. Yeats

Thomas Edison was just one successful person who may have battled a learning disorder as a child.

Leonardo da Vinci was a genius, but historians suspect he may also have struggled with a learning disability.

Obviously, not all children with learning disorders will grow up to be famous and successful—but there is no reason why they cannot grow up to be happy and productive. Unfortunately, however, if their difficulties are not addressed, many children with this disorder suffer from poor self-esteem. They are apt to be discouraged and frustrated in the school setting, and their frustration can lead to other problems. Since they find it difficult to succeed at the skills that teachers and parents tell them are so important for achievement, these children sometimes give up; some of them turn to delinquency or violence as a way to vent their frustration. Early diagnosis contributes to the successful treatment of learning disorders. No child should have to wait as long as Charlie did to get the help he needs.

The more opportunities a child has to practice successful strategies for coping with learning disorders, the more the child will get in the habit of performing these strategies automatically. It's a little like playing basketball: the more you practice your jump shots, the more easily the ball will fall through the hoop. When you've practiced enough, you don't have to devote as much attention to the mechanics. It's the same with playing a musical instrument—and it's the same with academic tasks like reading, writing, and mathematics.

Not every child will grow up to be a Thomas Edison or an Albert Einstein. But children with learning disorders *can* learn coping strategies. They may even have their own unique and creative slant on life to enrich their learning.

FURTHER READING

Brown, Dale S. *Learning a Living: A Guide to Planning Your Career and Finding a Job for People with Learning Disabilities, Attention Deficit Disorder, and Dyslexia.* Bethesda, Md.: Wobine House, 2000.

Cheatum, Billye Ann, and Allison A. Hammond. *Physical Activities for Improving Children's Learning and Behavior.* Champaign, Ill.: Human Kinetics, 2000.

Janover, Caroline. *The Worst Speller in Jr. High.* Minneapolis, Minn.: Free Spirit Publishing, Inc., 1995.

Levine, Mel. *A Mind at a Time.* New York: Simon & Schuster, 2002.

Lyman, Donald E. *Making the Words Stand Still.* Boston: Houghton Mifflin, 1986.

Mooney, Jonathan, and David Cole. *Learning Outside the Lines.* New York: Simon & Schuster, 2000.

Smith, Corinne, and Lisa Strick. *Learning Disabilities: A to Z.* New York: The Free Press, 1997.

Tuttle, Cheryl Gerson, and Penny Paquette. *Parenting a Child with a Learning Disability.* New York: Doubleday, 1993.

FOR MORE INFORMATION

ADD Anonymous
PO Box 421227
San Diego, CA 92142-1227
addanon@aol.com

ADDIEN ADDult Information Exchange Network
PO Box 1991
Ann Arbor, MI 48106
www.addien.org

ADD Action Group
175 West 72nd Street, 2nd Floor
New York, NY 10023
www.addgroup.org

All Kinds of Minds
www.allkindsofminds.org

CHADD (Children and Adults with Attention Deficit Disorder)
8181 Professional Place, Suite 201
Landover, MD 20785
www.chadd.org

Davis Dyslexia Association International
www.dyslexia.com

International Dyslexia Association
www.interdys.org

Internet Special Education Resources (ISER)
www.iser.com

Mental Health Net
adhd.mentalhelp.net/ and adhd.mentalhelp.net/

Schwab Foundation for Learning
www.schwablearning.org

Information on the Wilson Reading System may be found at:
    userpages.acadia.net/waldolva/wilson/wilson.html

Publisher's Note:

The Web sites listed on these pages were active at the time of publication. The publisher is not responsible for Web sites that have changed their address or discontinued operation since the date of publication. The publisher will review and update the Web sites upon each reprint.

GLOSSARY

automaticity: The condition of being automatic; in this case, learning the skills of decoding the English language so well that it becomes automatic.

bipolar disorder: A psychiatric disorder that causes extreme emotional highs and lows.

digraphs: Two letters that function together as one sound in the English language.

diphthongs: A complex vowel sound that involves gliding from one sound to another in the same syllable.

discrimination: To treat a person or group of people differently because of the category to which they belong (for example, an ethnic group or a disability).

due process: Legal, formal procedures that must take place, protecting a person from arbitrary action on the part of law enforcement officers.

dyscalculia: A mathematical disorder that involves unusual difficulty solving math problems and understanding math concepts.

dysgraphia: A neurologically based writing disorder that involves difficulties forming letters and writing within a defined space.

dyslexia: A language-based learning disorder that involves difficulty reading.

fine motor coordination: Control of the small muscles in the hands. Lack of fine motor coordination that makes writing, artwork, and other detailed handwork difficult.

GED: General equivalency diploma, accepted by some employers in place of a high school diploma.

graphomotor function: The motor skills and output used in the act of writing.

gross motor skills: Coordination of the large muscles in the arms, legs, and body. An individual who lacks gross motor skills will appear clumsy and awkward; athletics will be difficult for this person.

IQ: Intelligence Quotient. This number is assigned based on intelligence tests given to a person.

phonemene: The smallest measure of sound in words.

segmentation: Breaking up words into segments, a necessary skill learned in the Wilson Reading System.

self-advocacy: The act of supporting or pleading for one's own rights.

syllabify: Dividing words into syllables.

Tourette's syndrome: A disease that causes involuntary movements and uncontrollable utterances, including obscene language.

INDEX

BIOGRAPHIES

Shirley Brinkerhoff is a writer, editor, speaker, and musician. She graduated from Cornerstone University with a Bachelor of Music degree, and from Western Michigan University with a Master of Music degree. She has published six young adult novels, thirteen informational books, and scores of short stories and articles. She teaches at writers' conferences throughout the United States and does author presentations for classes from kindergarten through high school.

Dr. Lisa Albers is a developmental behavioral pediatrician at Children's Hospital Boston and Harvard Medical School, where her responsibilities include outpatient pediatric teaching and patient care in the Developmental Medicine Center. She currently is Director of the Adoption Program, Director of Fellowships in Developmental and Behavioral Pediatrics, and collaborates in a consultation program for community health centers. She is also the school consultant for the Walker School, a residential school for children in the state foster care system.

Dr. Carolyn Bridgemohan is an instructor in pediatrics at Harvard Medical School and is a board-certified developmental behavioral pediatrician on staff in the Developmental Medicine Center at Children's Hospital, Boston. Her clinical practice includes children and youth with autism, hearing impairment, developmental language disorders, global delays, mental retardation, and attention and learning disorders. Dr. Bridgemohan is coeditor of *Bright Futures Case Studies for Primary Care Clinicians: Child Development and Behavior*, a curriculum used nationwide in pediatric residency training programs.

Cindy Croft is the State Special Needs Director in Minnesota, coordinating Project EXCEPTIONAL MN, through Concordia University. Project EXCEPTIONAL MN is a state project that supports the inclusion of children in community settings through training, on-site consultation, and professional development. She also teaches as adjunct faculty for Concordia University, St. Paul, Minnesota. She has worked in the special needs arena for the past fifteen years.

Dr. Laurie Glader is a developmental pediatrician at Children's Hospital in Boston where she directs the Cerebral Palsy Program and is a staff pediatrician with the Coordinated Care Services, a program designed to meet the needs of children with special health care needs. Dr. Glader also teaches regularly at Harvard Medical School. Her work with public agencies includes New England SERVE, an organization that builds connections between state health departments, health care organizations, community providers, and families. She is also the staff physician at the Cotting School, a school specializing in the education of children with a wide range of special health care needs.

Franklin Pierce College Library

00152694

DATE DUE